Michael Horovitz

GROWING UP:-
SELECTED POEMS AND
PICTURES 1951-'79

Allison & Busby, London

First published in 1979 by
Allison and Busby Limited
at 6a Noel Street, London W1V 3RB, England

Copyright © Michael Horovitz 1979

Horovitz, Michael
    Growing up: selected poems and pictures 1951—1979
    I. Title
    821'.9'14   PR6058.0714G/   79-40015
    ISBN 0-85031-232-9
    ISBN 0-85031-233-7 Pbk

Printed in Great Britain by The Anchor Press Ltd
and bound by William Brendon & Son Ltd
both of Tiptree, Essex

Designed by the author, with reservations and revisions by Richard Adams.

Of this first edition, 50 signed & numbered copies have been inscribed with an extra original hand-drawn picture-poem by the author.

Here's a big thank you to all the editors and publishers of the magazines, newspapers, journals and anthologies in which many of these poems (& some of the pictures) first appeared — often in more primitive versions. As there have been so many, the specific acknowledgements that follow are restricted to the publications still in print and continuing at this time of going to press (& let's hope, hereafter): —

Akzente, Ambit, Aquarius, Arnold Bocklin, Art Monthly, Arts in Society, Bananas, The Black Box, Bombay Gin, Books (NBL), Caliban, Cherwell, Chuo Koron, City Lights Journal, Clare Market Review, Edge, Elysian, Evergreen, Folkways Records, Gargoyle, Global Tapestry, Granta, Hotcha, Hot Water, Isis, Jewish Quarterly, Joe DiMaggio, Labris, Lines, The Listener, The Littack Supplement, The Little Word Machine, the Live New Departures programme magazines, Mannanaun, Mars, Museum of Temporary Art, New Departures, New Style, New York Quarterly, 19, Oasis, One, Ord & Bild, Painted Bride Quarterly, Penumbra, Poetry Information, Poetry Project Newsletter, Poetry Review, Primer, Prism International, Resurgence, Samphire, Sandwiches, The Scotsman, Shady Side News, Stonecloud, Straight Lines, Three Sisters, TLS, Topolski's Chronicle, Tribune, Unmuzzled Ox, Undercurrents, Vogue, Vortex, and the Western Daily Press.

Acknowledgement is also due to M Horovitz's previous booklets under the *New Departures* imprint — Strangers, Leaves from a Book of Changes, and Love Poems; and to the anthologies —

Astronauts of Inner Space (Stolen Paper Editions), Children of Albion (& its imminent sequel), Experimentalni Poezie, A Festschrift for KFB, For Bill Butler, The Grove, The Healing of the Nations (Anglo-Welsh Review), Jazz Poems, Love Love Love, The New British Poetry, New Departures 'BIG HUGE' anniversary reunion anthology, PEN New Poems 1965, Pick Me Up, The Poets' Encyclopaedia (Unmuzzled Ox), A Tribute to Kenneth Patchen, Venice Poetry Company presents . . ., and Ver Sacrum.

Michael Horovitz also acknowledges that his 1977 Writer's Award from the Arts Council of Great Britain enabled him to take time out and complete this book, with much more care than could otherwise have been lavished.

The selection has been put together with a view to being read alongside the author's companion volume, an illustrated sequence of **Inter / City Poems** (*New Departures 12* — available from N Ds, Piedmont, Bisley, Stroud, Glos GL6 7BU).

This book is dedicated to the many friends who have helped inspire, collate and reproduce the works in it — & that includes you, readers unknown, if you in turn will make friends with some of them.

— And in special
to
R R H
F M H
and
A A H—

. . . & *Aah!* to my fellow poets & artists as well: meaning (not only my son's initials, but) may "The lineaments of gratified desire" shine upon you. — And likewise, on the following good people, without whose several & various contributions the total assemblage would be a sadder, and a duller thing:—

Richard Adams Anna Balogh Jonathan Barker David Batterham Laura Beck
Samuel Beckett Tom Bendhem Pete Brown Joe Collins Carry Court Natalie Deane
Michael Hastings David Hockney Marigold Hodgkinson Adam & Frances Horovitz
Rosi Horovitz John & Judy Horton Libby Houston Ozzie Jones Jane Kasmin
Alan Kitching Alan & Jean Lloyd Charlie Maclean Michele Mortimer Jenny Prior
Private Eye David Redfern Tony Rushton Ron Sandford Tessa Sayle
Lendal Scott-Ellis Geoffrey Soar Tom Stoppard Will Sulkin Vanessa Terry
Joe Weldon Heathcote Williams Jenni Williamson — all the gang at Allison & Busby, and anyone I've left out.

Photographs and Illustrations

The upper photograph on page 1, by Alfred Benjamin, depicts about half of the Horovitz family of 1946 (l to r): brother Martin, the author aged 11, eldest sister Selma, her daughter Roberta, Aba, Rosi, siblings Elsie & Felix (now Baruch). The lower photo on this page, by Bill Gardiner, is of Adam Albion & Michael Horovitz in the Cotswolds in 1974.

Both photos on p. 24 are of M H aged 5, in 1940; and on p. 25 (top, l to r) he's with his mother, 1936; with his father & niece, in the Gare du Nord, 1949; and with A L, first love, 1955. The shot below these on the same page is by Alan Parkin, and shows M H at an ambiguous moment, somewhere between would-be heroic action painting and near suicidal freaking out (of which kind there were many that year) on Soho rooftops in 1963.

The upper photo on p. 49, of sunlight on water, is by A R Lomberg. The swanscape beneath it is by Marigold Hodgkinson. The snap on p. 54 is by Bill Gardiner, of Frances Horovitz in 1976; and the other one of her, with Adam in 1973 (p. 94) is by Michael Horovitz; whilst the shot on p. 66 of the latter playing his kazoo in Missoula, Montana, 1977, is by Curt Walters.

Plus — nearly forgot: lower left 24 — Rosi H, early '30s; clouds on p.48 by Gabi Nasemann; p.68 — Bird and Monk below (by I dunno who), and upper shot of Monk by Valerie Wilmer.

All the other illustrations are by yours truly, "the author", except the following, to whom, again, my heartfelt thanks: —

David Hockney for the cover drawing, 1978; the drawings on pages 14 & 34 by the late Mal Dean (1960 & '68); the detail from one of Gustave Doré's marvellous engravings for *The Rime of the Ancient Mariner* (1875) 36; Ron Sandford's interpretation of the anti-war poem on p. 64; the 'brandyglass' version of *Hot Wine* by Rolf Gunter & Klaus Peter Dienst, from their magazine **Rhinozeros**, 1964, p. 71; and Blake's 1780 engraving of *Morning, or Glad Day*, on p. 84.

A few of the titles of my paintings may be found relevant or informative, in relation to the texts they accompany, e.g. —

Beauty and the Bug, 17; Execution, 33; Death Masque, 37; Hung-up with Strings, 45; Eve Blossom Nocturne, 61; 'I am white, but O! my soul is black', 72; Dizzy with Strings, 73; Old Bird with a Horn (multiplied drawing) 75; Resurrection of the Body (detail) 78 — the complete painting is reproduced across page 18.

The collage-poem *Catastrophe* on p. 70 features a jam session whose all-star line-up got so carried away, we shall not see its like again . . . *viz*, l to r:

I Stravinsky, nameless Black-*and*-white South African Gnoo, Anna Lovell aged 3, Yehudi Menuhin, Little Brother Lenin, Lionel Hampton, Bix, Solomon Schonfield and unidentified flying rabbi, Dick Heckstall-Smith on tenor, T Monk on hand, John Cage in angelic transport, Stan Tracey and Zephyrs, fronted by Shakespeare on bass, Douglas Gray pipes and St Louis Armstrong — NONE of whom ain't gonna study war no more: just sit back, and Imagine the music . . . .

CONTENTS

[*Note:* for those interested in chronology, development or degeneration, I've put the year(s) of composition of each poem. And I've added the names of the people — amongst the living and the living dead — to whom each poem is especially addressed or dedicated, for one reason or another.]

I — PRELUDES

Glove Song (of a cavalier or cock-happy bloke copping out under the strain of his conformist background's yoke) 6 — for Stevie Smith, R I P, 1967, '76. *Old Tyme Ballad* 7 — for Michael Irwin (who co-wrote its first version, in the school library) 1951, 1960. *Coldwater Lyric* 7 — for e e cummings, 1960. *Direct Communication* 8 — for S S, '61. *The Young Lochinvar's Come-uppance* 9 — 1968, '77. *The Cat that Copies Itself* 10 — '67. *The Changing Face of an Actress* 10 — for F H, '65. *Poesy — on the Mat* 11 — for Moran of Greek St, '63. *Song of The Egoist* 11 — for C L, '61. *Spiked* 12 — 1967/'69. *Theology* 13 — for dsh, 1960. *Nether Depths* 13 — for Wm Burroughs, Anthony Blond, & other family folk, '66. *Serpentine* picture-poem 13 — for Jackson Pollock & G C, 1961. *Look Ahead* 15 — for Wm Green & Will Morris, '59/60 & '77/78. *Retorts to Philistia* 16 — for Gertrude Stein, Kurt Schwitters & Ernst Jandl; for the freedom of art's sake's range; for Plurabelles to be . . ! 1968, '77/78. *english nocturne* 17 — for James Joyce & Godofredo Iommi, '61. *Resurrection of the Body* 18 — for N O Brown & Allen Ginsberg, 1963, '66, '77. *Ballade of the Nockturnal Commune* 20 — for the Incredible Stringband, for continuity of the 'love generation', '66/67 & '77/78. *'Leave the bright voices at the edge of the wood'* 21 — for Frances Horovitz (from whose poem 'Bird' the title-line is borrowed), TSE & Jn Ashbery, 1968, '77/79.

II — GROWING UP

Growing Up deferred 24 — 1956. *Nausée* 25 — for Sophie Tucker, J-P Sartre, & my parents, 1963. *Growing Up continued* 26 — for Jack Kerouac & William Golding, 1970, '77/78. *'The Question is — impossible: O Answer . . .'* 29 — '60/ 61. *A Primrose speaks* 30 — for Wm Blake & Kenneth Patchen, 1961. *Departing Spirits* 31 — for Walt Whitman & Alan Davie, '67 & '77. *the consumer society extorts our inner lives* 32 — for Dylan Thomas, 1968, '77/78. *Microscopic* 34 — '68. *Scream* 34 — '68. *Growing Up concluded (?)* 34 — for Samuel Beckett, Philip O'Connor, & Harry Fainlight, 1960. *Beginning to accept myself* 35 — 1967/'68 & '77/78.

III — DARKNESS AND LIGHT

ParadiCe 36 — 1960, '77/78. *Enlightenment* 38 — '67. *Birthday Poem* 38 — for Kathleen Raine, 1967, '77/78. *Listening to St Matthew's Passion* 42 — '68/78. *Everything looks so good in the window* 43 — 1960. *Tensions* 43 — for my bicycle of that era, 1959. *Hard by Old Jewry* 44 — for Ray Heavenstone & Bernard Kops, '59/60. *'Uccelli in Testa'* 45 — for Camus, Charlie Parker, Mark Hyatt, B S' Johnson, & all the others so sadly gone before their time, 1960, '62. *'meanwhile life outside goes on all around you'* 46 — for Pound & Bob Dylan, 1962, '78. *Notting Hill Windowscape* 46 — 1968. *Polyglottal Stop* 47 — for F H, also F & S Themerson, 1963/'65.

IV — SIGHTS AND SOUNDS

Evening (Hubris & Fall) 48 — for Bill Tucker, 1958/60. *reflections on the water* 49 — 1967 & '77. *overslept reflections on the cold/water music* 50 — for F H,

John Haag, & Roger Garfitt, 1977. *Fear and Relief* 54 — 1968. *"no birds / jingle / in the wind"* 54 — for F H, mid '60s. *A Solemn & Sensuous Musick* 55 — for F H, '76. *Highland Rhapsody* 56 — for all Scottish makars, 1967/69 & '74. *glimpse* 57 — for W C Williams, late '60s. *country life* 57 — for John Cage, late '60s. *Thatched* 58 — 1959. *End of the writing day* 58 — c. 1967.

V — SONGS OF THE SEASONS

"autumn's ex- / foliate heroes" 59 — something back to H Fainlight, for his autumn poems, 1967 & '77. Picture-poem: *Reminder* 59 — for Carlyle Reedy, '62. *A Newcomer* 60 — for Adam Horovitz, Thomas Wyatt, & Sidney Bechet, 1961. *primavera* 61 — for F H, & Dave Tomlin, 1967. *Summer* 61 — for John Clare, and Marcelle & John Papworth, '68. *A Ghost of Summer* 63 — '68/69 & reshaped (from a sonnet into a song) '77/8. *Autumn without end* 64 — for Rilke, Brecht — & for all the innocently fallen, 1958, '65, '70 & '78. *And the ignorant armies/let them eat — beautiful soup'* 65 — for Keats & Jeff Nuttall, 1968 & '78.

VI — JAZZ POEMS

Moving Pads 66 — 1967. *Sing Out* 66 — 1966. *Lies* 67 — for the English canon of canons & madrigals, & for Jimmy Yancey & the other fugal boogie-meisters, 1959 & '78. *Sea's Cape* 67 — for Ornette Coleman, Lol Coxhill, Ron Geesin, Ivor Cutler & Bill Gardiner, '76/77. *Thelonius* 68 — for Stan Tracey as well as Monk, 1958, '63 & '77. *Catastrophe* 70 — for Stella Bittleston, Dick Heckstall-Smith & all the other 'Live New Departures' musicians, 1960. *Hot Wine* 71 — for Cornelius Cardew, Anselm Hollo, & Kenny Graham, 1959/60. *Graffito from the Stone Age* 71 — for Gregory Corso (& his request in the milkbottle for "Penguin dust"!), '66 & '77. *Remembering the Stone Age* 72 — for Teddy Gordon & Julian Reeves, early/mid '70s. *Blank O'Clock Blues* 73 — for Adrian Mitchell (from whose play 'Tyger' the quatrain italicised in the middle of p. 74 is lifted . . .); & for the whole venerable tradition of black American blues from its famous & infamous exponents to good old Anon. Has gone through many versions between '68 & '78. *Back at the Club* 75 — for the Literary Commissars at the ACGB, 1959/'76; writ in '67. *Real High* 75 — for Pete Brown, '68. *Man-to-Man Blues Mantra* 75 — 1963/ '64. *fresh flowers surrounded us* 78 — for F & A H, '68/78. *Dream* 79 — for F H, '68. *"Damn your eyes — "* 80 — for F H, & Robert Creeley, 1961.

VII — LOVE POEMS

You 81 — for F H, mid '60s. *" . . . Is this really / a free love — "* 82 — for F H, '61/63. *Idyll / with shadows* 83 — for F H, 1970 & '77. *Glad Day* 85 — for F H, & G M Hopkins, 1966. *For Chagall / & my bride* 89 — '62. *Song* 89 — for F H & Jn Donne, '68. *"The most beautiful girl / in the world is an abstraction — "* 90 — for F H, & Brian Patten, c '69. *Remembering* 91 — for A L, '62. *Blessings* 92 — for F H, & all the Cohenim, 1967, '71 & '78. *Aubade on the beach* 95 — for F H, 1970; *Glove Song* (of an old soak or pig without a poke) 95 — for A & F H, W B Yeats, and John Masefield, '78/79.

VIII — CODA

'There's a hitch in these haiku': Lines occasioned by the worst winter since the year of his birth 96 — for E J Thribb (17), 1979.

— Now read on ! —

I· PRELUDES

(& juvenilia, jeux d'esprit, cameos, picture-poems, paintry, squibs, keynotes, performance pieces)

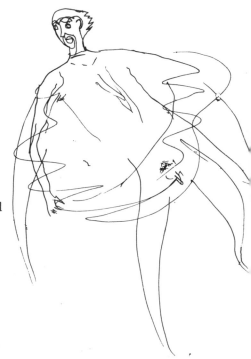

G l o v e
S o n g

Is there a face
            in the sun
— A stone
        in the ice,
Is this the safe
            to blow?

And is there a trace
    of your breath
                in the cloud
— Or shall I fly
straight through it
                and go

To lands
        where sunshine
    might snow
                forever a-
                roly-poly-o - ?

— I don't know
    — in two minds
        — best say   No:
(It might
        turn out
                a bad show)

. . . Whilst the egg
                in the head
        — It is hatching
                    hatching

        The socks
                on the feet
            — They are matching
                        matching,

6

Old Tyme Ballad

Lady Ermyntrude was sitting
   with her ladies knitting
Near by

When all at once she beheld
   a knight in the feld
Nigh

He hove to with a whistle
   and raised his thistle
High

And a rose he brought her
   as he caught her
Eye

She waved her 'kerchief
   trusting he'd lief
Try

To retrieve it
                  if she dropped it
But when she did
                  — he hopped it

   — I often wonder

. . . .
Why?

COLDWATER LYRIC

SING ——
   a song of spring
cries the land
Lady   viewing his
UNsprung mattress
   —See
         how they are busy
buds popping
   wasps buzzing
      worms squirming
      birds squealing
      melody of flowers
      in the beds, and
   one lonely privet
hedgeing
the boarder —

7

Direct Communication

(poet to secretary)

why paint your mouth
that pillarbox red
if you don't want
my letters popped in

only mail* can be expressed
with any degree of certitude
as to its delivery
to another

but I tell you I love
you can't you
understand I'm crazy
about the way you lick

stamps —

* — The decline in postal services during the years since this was written casts an inescapable shadow over the faith maintained by my second stanza. However, not wishing to renounce it irretrievably, I hereby dedicate the whole considered trifle to the GPO — & expect nothing less in return than an immediate restoration of their total credibility.

If this is not forthcoming, a movement will have to be founded, urging all men & women of letters and all secretaries to other (more lickerish) pursuits than writing, reading, or the unpalatable — but ever more exorbitant — application of philately.

Yea: let the ecstacies of oralism forever unbound be posted at every door that wants them. That the Babel of dead, delayed or misdirected linear missiles be overcome; and the tongues of all God's children freed — with palpable pleasure filled . . . with ripeness to the core, of deepest desires all got — somewhere!

The Young Lochinvar's Come-uppance

in our time

"Then all the Males conjoined into One Male, & every one
Became a ravening eating Cancer growing in the female . . ."

(Blake — 'Jerusalem' pl. 69)

Thursday, Thor's day — what if there's
Thunder blunder and hell's bells to pay
Or no pay, no hit — no smartass getaway —
What about the Tarot . . . the Ching . . . the omens
— Ach . . . to heck with the omens   — But
What's this, a beautiful chick
Walks straight through my reverie — wheeling
A baby —   and there was a Me
Riding high with stardom close by
Pushed smack in the deep end
Of the slimy moat —   .
Her grip lassoos my throat
She nips — I hack back . . . Mmmm
She tastes
delicious —
I lunge further
To get in deeper
Crying Oats Oats Oats
— Till her eyes yell back
Use your loaf you oaf
As she bites my tongue
But lets the rest of me go
— So I eat her toe
Yet she flounces away
And I can't say my say
The typical end
Of a stormy day.

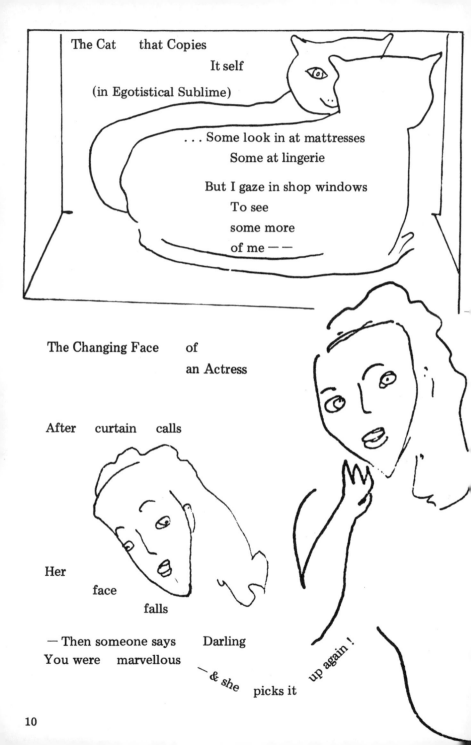

The Cat   that Copies

          It self

    (in Egotistical Sublime)

         . . . Some look in at mattresses
              Some at lingerie

         But I gaze in shop windows
         To see
         some more
         of me — —

The Changing Face   of
                  an Actress

After   curtain   calls

Her

      face

         falls

— Then someone says   Darling
You were   marvellous

             — & she   picks it   up again !

Poesy   on the Mat

You said:
    Regal
he sate
as of ginger
bread   and snow
    compounded

but *he* wishes he were made

                              of Kit-E-Kat

Ratiocinatory
Song of
The Egoist

                    (Beckett's Pozzo in mind, also
                       Schopenhauer's aesthetic transcendence
                         — "Nothing
                                        is more real
                              than nothing")

        I devour
what is before me.

        I sometimes ache for
what is beyond me —

Tho — it might be said,
            since nothing is before me
            I have — nothing

Yet — since nothing is beyond me,
            I want for nothing:

        So, if I look back
at what I have wanted,

        I can be well satisfied
with what I have got.

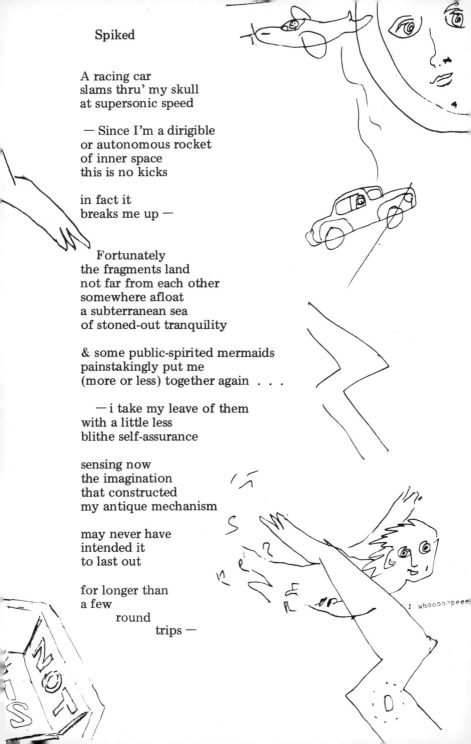

Spiked

A racing car
slams thru' my skull
at supersonic speed

— Since I'm a dirigible
or autonomous rocket
of inner space
this is no kicks

in fact it
breaks me up —

      Fortunately
the fragments land
not far from each other
somewhere afloat
a subterranean sea
of stoned-out tranquility

& some public-spirited mermaids
painstakingly put me
(more or less) together again . . .

      — i take my leave of them
with a little less
blithe self-assurance

sensing now
the imagination
that constructed
my antique mechanism

may never have
intended it
to last out

for longer than
a few
            round
                  trips —

! whooooopeee

Theology

God's in His Heaven

Creating . . . Earth —

When He gets down here

He's going to raise
                    — Hell!

Nether Depths

See here now —

the roots I'll expose

        — the family tree

has dirty toes . . . .

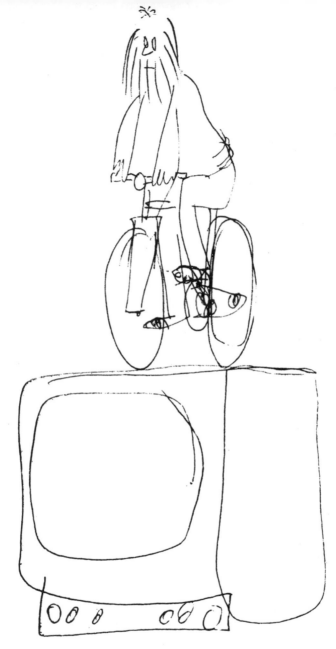

(Mal Dean realized this small vision in the course of a reading at which I'd announced the initial inspiration of *Look Ahead* opposite — the sight, during the heyday of action painting happenings, of "an artist cycling on the television" . . . . . .)

Look Ahead

Our toes are ahead of us — they have grown out of us

Our nails are ahead of our toes — we can't reach to cut them

Our hammers are ahead of our nails — they strike
    like underpaid lightning

Our sickles are ahead of our hammers — shape of our hammer toes

Our televisions are ahead of our cinemas — our films are because
    we don't use good toothpaste
    state and church fight tooth and nail
    whilst producers forge ahead of viewers

Our commercials are ahead of our patrons —
    all is peddled

Our cycles are ahead of our tricycles and our trickles are
    our fashionable works of art
    trickled   by cyclists   on paint

Our best cyclists are our worst painters and

Our best painters are worse than our worst cyclists —

Our worst cyclists are ahead of all our painters
    put together — save the painters become cyclists
    and that's what they've done —
    every day more painters are taking up cycling
    and daily they are discovered
    biking up the strand —
    sponsored they swerve through swirls of paint
    dribble ahead of trolleys trams trombones —
    start brushing their feet with toothpaste
    that the Tour de France is gunged to a standstill
    whilst cinemas clean up with the masses at bingo
    and the backsliding punter lies down with the telly —

Our piledriver toes hammer furiously on motorcycles
    but the hammers are sliced by sickles
    struck hard by

Our frames our nails catch up with our toes till at last
    we're in —
    we find our — teeth
    fully grown

    footballers

Retorts to Philistia

Art continues to get a bad press from intellectuals who are often (only) articulating their own thwarted creativity. Plato spoke of artistic inspiration as madness and, though he conceded that this contains veritably divine and healthful elements, banished its exponents from the ideal state. Freud bracketed it with other ludic and philosophic manifestations as "anal eroticism" which, coming from him, is an unpleasant and dismissive term. And the influential Scottish commentator Fyfe Robertson saw fit to pronounce the first (1977) Hayward Annual exhibition of innovative painting, sculpture and performance art, a fart in the public eye. " — Their lunacies", he said on TV, "are phoney art. You can condense these two words into one which has the proper flavour of contemptuous derision, Phart" . . .

[My closing citation is filched from the pen of Our Vater, which art in Heaven: the ultra-cunninglinguish (I mean, oral) artifisher James Joyce.]

> The Republic and The Laws of Plato
> dropped the arts like a hot potato,
> missing out on the Arse Poetica
> you too might look up and into, Herr Doktor
> — there's a lot more to it than bánal erotica.
> And there's no real reason art should bring to mind
> a puritanical retreat from the human behind
> — nor yet, auld Robbie, this piddling grind
> about phoney or noisome breaks in the wind.
>
> Farts and belches come in twos
> like the Christians and the Jews —
> but *if* it come, Art is *not*   unnatural
> (no more   than they are
> but often —) more like leaves
> to the tree of life

> ART . . . *IS*

— not "phart" — or
art is not all fart — till
art is not at all fart, then
art is not at all far — &
art is not at all f —
art is not at a —
art is not a
art is no
art is n
art is
art
—
a
?

. . . art is not fat
art is not thin
art is well fed
in the loony bin . . . . . .

        Art is yes — och — aye, i e —
is poster-peelings, a way
of seeing, sometimes a mess
  — call that messy art,
it may be far out, for art is long
whilst time flies and science goes wrong
  — so why add fuel (have a heart)
to the massive dreary anti-art chart
of the Great Municipal Public dustcart
which would much rather chuck it as rubbish or Phart
than have to wake up and actually start
thinking, enjoying — playing a part
and working at it, drat it

. . . to find
aah! — Art
thou
with it
now?   Then rejoyce — dada lives
      and mama, baba live — playing, praying
      in good voice : —
Loud,
heap miseries upon us
yet entwine our arts
with laughters low

                    english nocturne

                        no cricket you
                 moth moth
                    bat yr wings

            till you're happy

                        as a century —

RESURRECTION OF THE BODY

spells
   buds . blossoms
      bugs   into butter
        flies
— death alone   dies   in the face
    of hot peace showers
flowering   unquestioned   space

   bird's in his heaven
   all's well with the worm
earth glows   continuous —
   a big snake curls up
the aisle — swishes   & swings
to the electric   rock   of ages
the massed ark choir sings
& the animal   congregation   digs
its wondrous   sensate   infinity

   — pigs   dance with pigs
fish are jumping   heifers humping
   looney mice nibble
   at a vast moony cheese
   (traps   trap   traps)

          bride   groom   & babe
inter
     twine their blissful limbs
tasting the orb — man
                         ball
          to womb
                    head —
darting the root
     hugging the trunk
          kissing the buds
               fearless shaking
               the tree of life
catching at — crunching
& sucking to the core
     the apples
     of knowledge
          as they fall
          to
               each other's
eyes

          — you can tell
     from those weird signs
     & subtle colours
     god's somewhere
          in on the scene
     but he's letting the devil
     sit in his throne
&   breathing deep   each
     & every
               one else
picks himself up
     — finds a fit place
blessed by
               her own
                         creation
     — digs each
               their piece
of garden

     where every
                    body understands
seeded   in mutual   tenderness
     joined —
               many hands
make light work
                    — make shine
the peaceable kingdom   flesh

Ballade of the Nockturnal Commune

[to be read — or better, heard — in mind of the tune I've invented for it, which is partially drawn from those of 'Lord of the Dance' and Bob Dylan's 'As I went out one morning': the italicised refrains are meant to be spoken or sung *twice over* —]

On the night that immemorial
cats set off as oft —
bats bestrid the cavern
and the belfry-toppled croft:

Now as voles they lay a-dying
and willow herb round swang,
stars envelop'd in mist now
owls turned over and sang

— Warm bodies curled, salt juices swathe
blent souls in tender of kin
and as day breaks the shell
of pale moon's waning egg
                        — the glad
            lover's leap
lepp'd in —

The evergreen lovers of leap ear
they made love, and they sank to sweet sleep
    — *stars cross lines with the sun now*
    owls turn over in sheep

And silverblue cornflowers cluster,
the ripening wheatgerm hears
the spaces of love truly felt now
    dissolve the far gone years

with the light of ancient springs to guide
lost minds
                to cool ease
                        in their glide —
jets of spring-powered
        joysticky seedspinning planes
take their leaves, leaving newborn refrains: —
dying leaf, blossom swirling tail-spun lives
drown their grief, leaving greenyellow stains

On the wings of song purgatorial
    — gnats flitted oft aloft —
bird-calls dappled the forest
and our love the arboreal croft.

" — Leave the bright voices at the edge of the wood

". . . all they talk of is films and clothes"

— Selling lines' Newspeak and wrap-up
jingle scrapes the snip-tun'd ear
so numb it hardly notices — and when
it's dock leaves stroke the palms of feet
the question "Isn't it only hands have palms"
elicits flip-type answers such as
"Dates have psalms".   — But psalms unsung,
answers branding paradise a childhood dream
forever lost; and the fleeting office windowscape
of vast blue summer skies we can't dive into
but intensifies the loss.   Our senses
got confused by fool's gold-digging where —
   O where the candyfloss that pinkly whirled
in infancy's fair and truly happy simulacrum
of the 'important' grown-up universe?

   — Still there, but slots back only
at the same appointed public holidays
 — routine of fading memories revived by
witnessing 'the other half', the 'rising
generation' — by watching others
glimpsing cameos of what (might have) happened
to oneself . . .   Foraging over the hills,
prematurely (— else yahboo to maturely) bent
on Production, lines of purpose (cripes)
 — disdaining
      the petticoat-flaring merrygoround
   & those teenage jazz-age jam session riffs
of endless Sunday sunshine lives
where cool cats sat on garden walls
and chicks went 'all the way' with you
(from squirrels & bears to Baby Roo
   — that's) what ever happens
   to all that
                  . . . The discovery of
                  Electricity
& now —
Instant organ-thunders jab the spine,
the glory groups pound gutty grooves
and feed back wave on shrilling wave of
   wordless wanted news
coiling eager loose submissive heads
to jerk and nod and rock
and oft-times zonk — giddy, and gone for real
in the name of insurrection's dervish dance . . .

But I would for real to the woods my love
and frolic amongst the poppy sheaves,
lie us down . . . give ear to starling wings
    to their chirrupings at cottage eaves —
intertwine and in our own good time
and place and way explode; and lull
    lullabye one another, recline
in the long grass — singing
madrigals, gather berries for wine

   . . . I would rather do that
than shovel on down this coalhole
gauntlet run of career and know-how the
view gets so blurred turning dream
to nightmare, dragging drays of
    individually (unquote) mass-consumed
       prizey carat ice-scoops of megapolis;
                                Moloch-mine
    of softer blow job hunting and hoarding,
       of Teasmade alarm-call relevations
— birdless pill days, 'lived' through — how?   God,
some profiteering machinery knows — lived 'on', by
the means, with the jabs of . . . any laid back /ground
?music's umbilical switches of sound (brash patter
making palatable — whatever's 'in': barbarian-arrivist
oldyoung rasp of punk, claw-toothed drill that closes in to kill
    each nerve exposed in turn — dying of the anaesthetic
if not the virus, of drossen oldies
— at best, like 'Bábylu-uv') churned out, jockeyed
 . . . 'through' the underpass;   and kept

                        down —

        choiceless pit ponies
      powerless cast
   to the mercies of carrion cars
bearing businesses & bands of renown
   — no angels

            for angels are out of fashion in town
               though angelic beings survive —
            dumb clowns, princesses divine
            in gaudy shawls turning life into
            theatre and theatre to life

                        — You a princess, I a clown
                        sharing unspoken yearning
                        for so much unspeakably more
                        than ever could grow in one garden
         . . . yet any garden does
      no less
         than what we make of it —

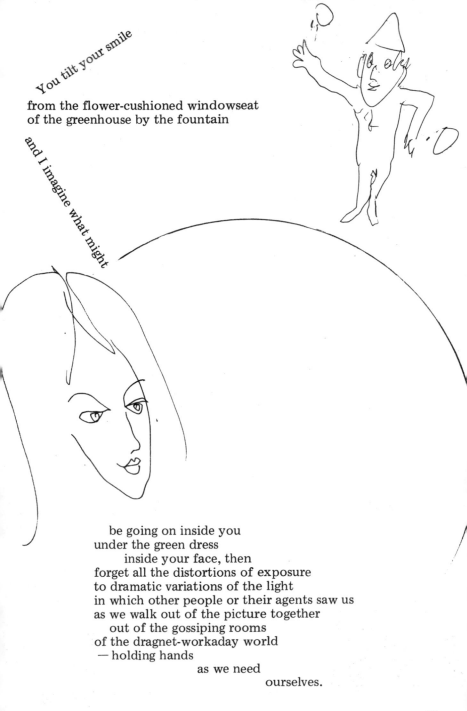

You tilt your smile

from the flower-cushioned windowseat
of the greenhouse by the fountain

and I imagine what might

be going on inside you
under the green dress
inside your face, then
forget all the distortions of exposure
to dramatic variations of the light
in which other people or their agents saw us
as we walk out of the picture together
out of the gossiping rooms
of the dragnet-workaday world
— holding hands
as we need
ourselves.

II- from GROWING UP (a sequence)

Growing Up
(deferred)

all alone in the shop
i am five years old

the moon is bright
the leaves bright green

birds are sleeping
the air is quiet

quietly the curtain waves
the boats sailing out to sea

in an early morning the
wind blowing billowing hard

the ship is big and the
books are good and

stories are told but . . . Oh
Great! — here's Mummy

— yesterday she went away
and it was hard to take

her place

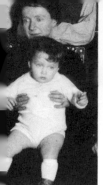

Nausée

The further I go from you
   mother
    father, the harder
the journey back :

First was loving — the wind. Now daily
   caring
    bearing
nausea, the rack —

nightly menaced — cloud forests that
   lower
    each hour
to crack

this eggshell of a mind.
   Premonitions
    apparitions
of madness, and the ripe years I lack —

"School days are the unhappiest in the whole span of human existence.   They
are full of dull, unintelligible tasks, new and unpleasant ordinances, brutal
violations of common sense and common decency."

(H L Mencken — 'Travail')

"Growing up's wonderful if
        you keep
            your eyes
                closed tightly,
    and if you grow up
        take your soul with you
            nobody wants it —

. . . . . . he's going to learn
how to lie correctly, how to lay correctly,
how to cheat and steal in the nicest possible manner . . ."

(Brian Patten — 'Schoolboy')

The best thing about school
was hols —

    Knees up
                in haystacks of memory . . . . . .
        — went limp every time
the starting pistol, bellsprung goad
ambition to make one's mark
groped for footholds
                at the headland
    — slippery grains!
        And recurrent panic fears
of being cast adrift forever — like the cruel reality
(frog-marched to the top board, pushed in
        and left
                for drowned
        — to oneself — the
        blind breathless
        stonebodied drop
                out of all that was known)
were emergencies too private
to clang the conch for.
                But another, certain summer
            returns to mind, you came to delight
            in that solitary secret
                    blue pool

early stumbled on by chance
on the run
from a hide-&-seek patrol

                    — scooped in the rock
                  between peaks way beyond
where last night's hard-won castles fell
and before the loom of careerist rewinds   you
   swam a little

             more easily

                each morning
 — glid — a new charm'd life
     eluding the monsters of
     unlimited   ungraspable
     underwater space
                — found your natural
                      depth — at one
     with the flow —   effortless, exulting
     the pristine sun-rippled brilliance

             . . . before the others'
            clamouring   competitions   con-
fused you   tried to

follow that call   and forget
                              the scenes
     unmade   — years seemingly wasted   looking
back   and measuring   forward — revising —
or merely insuring — 'results' — a Place, then another
on Big Brother's conveyor-belts to the routine pursuit
of prepacked life-bait: status / money / girlfriend(s) —
wife / 'n' kid(s) to follow with more or less exotic perks on tap,
tv & mortgaged shelter — before whose beckoning
guilt-edged shadow the imagination
caved in, mostly — at best contrived a semblance
of discreet ingestion, one slept   days'
end   over studied   end — only dreaming — *ideas*
of fulfillment . . . fruition . . .   'a l l   w a y s'

     . . . . . . only always
                         more —
even now (more than ever) the pattern clogs:
money
changes   hands
          join   — power
                    freaks   war
                              locks —   peace
                                              opens
     & then   the big payola
                         — food   fills
     — pleasant vacuum   of vac   (though that way
     middle aged fatness lay   — it was also)
mountaineers   earning their glory

     . . . till we came down
     from the best
     of free-spirited days,
     youth hostel hitching — high on the road
     with dharmic 'peak experience' scalped
     & sternly stashed under senior scout belts —
to feel every bump
     of oil sardine lunches
toiling about
     in the belly's
     slosh barrel
     — like beercans
     in a waterlogged
     haversack

The Question is   — impossible

O Answer . . .

What you call
Mind, Knowledge
I call love —
Understanding   snowed

. . . till I learned
to Prepare for exams
'Think' like trams
and Wheel it about — Let
nothing   leak out

. . . and now the light years
seem frozen over
all I seek
as I follow the sun
is to break
to that peace of
no mind, no beginning

for some
         one
              —every
                   where
the universe is   a new flower

 — opening

and closing

    — and opening
    anew

(However: "A flower has no power — only we,
who look after it" . . .   (Herbert Marcuse)

The Path of A
Primrose

Soft leafwomb unfurls
my yelloween song

. . . i grew up with the grass by night
and nearly took fright
seeing starlings sip dew
from the buttercup mead

but their water'd lips prime
the day of my light

. . . i glimpsed a white star-spray
surging the hedgerow

and forget-me-not, ladysmock
wafting in the breeze —

a timid mouse darts near whispering
the plough stole my tail
and gave it over to a farmhand
who chucked it aside
                    as of no account
for his horse to get bellyache
and reward his master with blear bad service

. . . sisterly celandines spared by the blade
swing a new tail together

but mousey scampers off to a puddle
splosh and squeaks sad suds
at their smiling heads —

the mossy beds all about here
beam with my familiars

. . . our gold pollen swells
plush pride of the nursery

till i curl up to sleep
and dream the thorns
off the wild rose on earth

from my prim heaven —

Departing Spirits

Turn it over —
One new leaf
After another

Comes the dawn
They've grown old
— they die.

Night fall — and
   I'm at it
   yet again

Singing and dancing
Awake and agape
To the celestial music
They seem to make

Just by floating
Or creeping around

Grass-
     hopping
the dispassionate ground
— Shifting rhythms
in the wind

— and especially
to those that fly
away   without a sigh —
aspire
  far higher
    than the man-
ball,
    root
       and tree
           of life
   from which
     they came —

the consumer society extorts our inner lives

*(for Dylan Thomas, for loss
of innocence)*

The sea was golden like your hair
Years after you first
Burst in
Out of nowhere
Like the fabled Birth of Venus
To tear open the dusty window
Of my lonely ingrown lassitudes and longings

I'd just started working on that beach
Deck-chair attendant
I'd been laughing at the television
For several weeks
When they came and took it away
— They said the next week they'd come
And take me away

There was nothing left in the fridge
Where we'd come to
Trying
To keep our love
Vacuum sealed
— The light gone dead
— Your absence
The wages of bad faith
Switched it so's   — I swear
It flickers **On**
When I *close* the door

Play with me
You said
So I did
And it was everything
The best songs celebrate
— Till the job way of death
With its '*Look* alive
In the back row there'
Pronounced the permanent
Eclipse of our sun

I couldn't raise an eyelid —
They carted off my bones
But my soul is still in detention
Writing lines of lost childhood
Over and over

Whilst the girls and boys
Run out to play
And in again
Two by two

   The ark of tradition
The palace of wisdom
The lotus of enlightenment
Hold me in thrall
 — Still the stud
Wants to ball

   Then a fury
Of husbands and wives
Steals into the secret
Palpitating chambers
Of earthly and blushless
Eternal delights
      — And casts
   All goodness
   To the flood

Where wild beasts recoil trembling
From the lust for blood

                 To answer with their lives
                 (Slabbed on the altars
                 Of civilised man's
                 Thrice daily religion

      — Or with luck only trapped
      To pace behind bars
      For the entertainment
      Of his fatted family)

No release
From hung-up tensions
Slavery and sacrifice
Year on habit-stained year

            . . . Comes the peace
         Mind dreamed
            Would awake it
               For joy

      And opens
               the hill
            That swallows
                  the boy —

MICROSCOPIC

— What does the inner eye
actually in this case show?
— A set of deeply embossed
leaf stencils the apprehension
of some awesome presence
watching above my right shoulder
no outlines only a dazzle
ochres and greens and yellows
and the pale purple of Suchard Milk
Chocolate wrappers fond memory
   whirring straight up
   my youthtime's alp —

SCREAM

     as that Edvard Munch painting on the bridge
        the very air — all of existence taken up
     in the single shared terror —
             that we have to
    cross the screaming bridge & take up residence
       in the black fortress of the abyss —

Growing Up

(concluded?)

He ran
 hard
  down the misty
  alley
   to catch up
    the footsteps
     round the corner

   but when he
   got there he
   heard them
   die   away
  nothing
  but echoes
of
  his
    own —

BEGINNING TO ACCEPT MYSELF

— beyond evoking any THEM to explain my wounded look
nor brandishing stigmata to the blandishments of magpies
deliberately untopical only just susceptible
of becoming . . . saleable jailable clubbable suckable
but because I choose it, not live up to any image
. . . decibels fade sunflickering past riffs of rag decades
a real unconditioned me takes shape, takes time to
mount its self-made mind, jocundly amble it, trot, gallop
— leap . . . over the hedge that cordons in the pukka racetrack
— bypass the steeplechase of Britain, decline
the onerously obstacular grovelling course to honours
— stuff the paper-hat applause whose slime sticks fast:
unseen unlicked arses tighten ranks draw in
    I got *no* ticket to ride
but I don' care
— the chairman hums, and haws — smooth hands proffer
gift-horses, nosebag rewards — another drag good man
at the gumptious gurgling waterpipes of peace
— yes please but must I therefore swallow also
army state and the whole caboodle
the regular norm the proper form, eschewing what's Not On
. . . bowing cowed in horror of nearly doing that which is not done?
I'd rather drown in dope fling out hope singing sink
on a broken wing, glean from random rhyme a think out of time
and mean what I say beyond the crime
of playing the world's worn games
abusing the birthright of body's rapture
hubristic, heedless of soul's anguish, mind's minding
— for I like it here — in my own real mind
I like to think —
               is that of —
                       my own real world
— not because it's safe and dry
because it's not — it's open, wide, to
all physical mental spirit feel
and no beyond no more

III - DARKNESS AND LIGHT

ParadiCe

[on first taking mescalin]

"If I feel physically as if the top of my head were taken off, I know that is poetry"

(Emily Dickinson in a letter)

"If the doors of perception were cleansed every thing would appear to man as it is, infinite"

(Blake — 'The Marriage of Heaven & Hell')

New skies alight in perfum'd dazzle
weightless green again —
no I — where went
the ground all one   electric
Aaaah the fierce energy in those motorcycles
— A milkbottle flute
pierces clouds of indigo
and scarlet lake guitars
erupt their excalibur
kaleidoscope of rainbows
flecked with phosphorescent manna
Walk now   brave
this blinding   white sun —
Perspectives
all doors opened   Quietly
voices trickle through
little feet through
the floor   Fingers
sift silt from clay
between the tiles
feeding worms
the eavebirds' playthings
Domestic ranges wilde —
i see   what I never have seen

Yet   know it will go from me
— I want too much
to grasp and hold   the key
turn over to others as if
from me   I reach out
to clasp and know
the beams of love
dissolve in my hand
fall-out of the damned
of nations —
Man's covenant   with the earth
and air   betrayed
The radiance turns to hail
I pace a crazy pavement joyless
    above is
        atomised
      sections of the
world   gone
    grey
brought down
Trapped in my image
Mine owne —

Halls of anguish

Mirrors of trembling

Enlightenment

is

sometimes

breathing

the street lamp

out

at dawn

and reading

between

the branches

Morning meditation

for Kathleen Raine's birthday

. . . as far as I know
is not very far
— dawn glows slow
in an old parked car

as far as I know
the earth is flat

. . . crescent : city : moon
— and there is light

incandescence
                through vapours
welling
        from ancient springs
spearless stars
                original   sun
rising   pink
            & gold
                & bright

. . . clarity and grace
— your lovely face
beckons my soul
to fly to its place

— cast again
into the belov'd
labours of art, to sift
true grain from the chat
                    and see
the light within my head
and the light without
a single
            fourfold
                        unity

    Hear, O London
thine own   lustrous
multicoloured voices raised
in jazzhalla jubilee, milkvans rattle
on by whilst all-night revellers straggle
and stomp with timbrel, flute & metal string
their brazen orgy to the lees   twitching
up & down & round the momently glistering
grasses and steps and stones of
this high day's quenchless
ghetto party-charged streets
and garden squares
and arbours of Notting Dale
— great trees of life through
eyes of leaves see
the same perennial changes
year on year.   Beams
of vision
            rinse the senses —
spatter fresh dreams
on corroded slum walls
& guide my hands
as early birds awoken
                    clatter
quicken'd and exultant
back at this

. . . discovering, writing
                to you

another america — united states
of being, body not a clumsiness
closed in — "shell" of bone
itself hallucination —
inner life instinct with
prismatic calligraphy
of root, branch
earth and sky
 — universe felt — known
as square no longer now but
sphere

          . . . Imagine it, say
all an orange, cut in half —
there across the centre
lies the ground we tread
& call "horizon"
                    — we adorn
this seeming all, visibly unbounded
surface — yet supernal domes
of upper air envelop us
                         beneath the skin
 — the living and the dead
in mutual aura, the circle is
complete

          & yet — how
greedily we snatch, scratch
tear at flesh
            with nails — desperate
to hammer home desire, scoop up
the cream of anyone's workaday pickings
 — drive
        mind back, spirit on, to make out,
rake in, that ends meet
and more — O so exhaustively
gut, gorge — squeeze
life's juice

          . . . I suck
the orange
            & I'm stuck
with the rind

— till I come
                 to unwind,
reflect
        without rage
                 on a humble
breathing
                 poetic
                         page
 — set down the abyss
and the knowledge
of every age

. . . that outside and within
this open cage
of "our" globe, of heaven
on earth (for that *is*
where we live — you —
ancient sky, futurity
in a dragonfly darting,
Frances and I
 — the blue bopper's high,
bluebottles brought low
and the underground worm)
myriad galaxies
continue spinning
(and minstrels singing
It is not dying
. . . *It is beginning* —)

    What more to endyte
than wish you the strongest
winds of inspiration
wind you libation
to pour forth in song
Blake-happy returns
of that immortal hour
when stone begat flower —

when your emanation
on Albion's spaces lit

 — newborn
in the void :

                Eternity is
in love
        with the productions of time

Listening to St Matthew's Passion

a stillness   a centre   a man
gold banners stream in sunlight
snow drops scarlet   threading white
   Christ's blood streaming
   good men's plight —

what bird is that   stretches out
   its insistent single note   cutting
   across the hot black evening

— calling me from dream of bliss
on earth to conscious realisation
of such dream beyond the note

   of lyricism only

   where i am now is green   alive
and promises clear water   and fresh light
to see   and bathe our wounds   tomorrow
   yes   you — green
   of grass   and green out of blue
and yellow — white of page — gold of sun
   red of fire   and here is ears

open to that infinite recurring note
   twittering home   the coming of night
the waning of light

— indifferent   to the passing   clamour of
years ideas empires reputations
   — literature — a line
   snatched from time — scampering
in vain   to survive the gentlest breeze
the kindliest howl
               of mad dog's desire —

sleep after the first
awakening is never the same

the grass drank deep in the night
rust thickens, mists descend
in the long night

no good that
trying to catch up on dreams
straining the eyes shut
fighting the dayglow — no, up

to swerve through the dawn clearings
unlock the throat of early birds
into street games — the greens, and

the gross net traps —

                Tensions

            A leaf
                  pinioned
                        in the mesh

        struggles
            like a moth
              to fly

                    — No: it is
                    the wind
                          that struggles

            The madcap
                  driver
        accelerates
                  his wirecutters

*"Yes: She fell four flights

. . . Her old man drew up just after
carrying a rabbit, the trefa thing
floppy ears hanging low, ragged
fur and legs — all freshly
gutted for the oven.   He danced up
jaunty for cheers — hadn't been back
since years but *Hallo, I'm here —*
Light the gas and lay the table —
    Where are you dear? Dead
silence —   then to himself he muttered:
    What happens to wives?   I should have
'phoned — I wonder . . . did she take
a lover?   Or — what are those
— long black cars   eeling
out of the narrow grey street
— What?   A Shiva —
    Who?   — My God, tell me — who
died?   It seems tactless
shouting at us weeping women
and our men with torn lapels,
swart growths, the ash-stains everywhere
— but he has to know, poor wretch:
    . . . *Dressmaker upstairs.*
    — Oh no — no — ai . . . My love —
my wife . . .   And you mourn her?   Were you
her friends?   How long had she
been religious?
    I have wasted my life
he said.   We never saw him again — "

---

* *Note:* the speaker (recollected many years later) is
a beturbaned Buba akimbo in her Petticoat Lane
doorway, circa 1960.

'Uccelli in Testa'

"Life is a disgusting riddle, but we can ask harder ones, was the Dadaist attitude. To many intelligent men at this time, suicide seemed to be the one remaining solution to the problem of living, and Dada was a spectacular form of suicide, a manifestation of almost lunatic despair."

(David Gascoyne — 'A Short History of Surrealism')

to have birds in the head is
    to be a little mad they say

so many same different things
    as   suicide is the only remaining

solution to the problem of life or
    suicide   is the only remaining problem

of life worth bothering about   when
    his car crashed into the tree the philosopher

was left with only death and its problems
    some people do things   others think about

doing them   or yield — driven — to routines
    like   in a mad world what is sanity   for

drivers : THIS IS IT   for the religious
    there is a world   to come

and some   there is no words
    have birds   in the head

"meanwhile life outside goes on all around you"

the hive is overpopulated
what a lot of daffodils
to set before   a busy king

the faking and framing   pyramids
money   a sorrow without
                                    leaves

only when he's dead
will he to his bed
beneath the trees

                          all vanities'
          ends   forgotten
no fearful darkness
there

              when god said
there was light

                    you could see
          for miles

Notting Hill Windowscape

blue grey
pregnant sky
delivers
          its waters

& the cloud is lifted
from this city
garden   square

ho   the deep greens
   surf deeper
   and greener
and the lighter
   glade shines
leaf flesh afresh
in sylvan sheen

— strangely
soundless   interval
   of evanescent
afterburst   stillness

Polyglottal Stop

once O once
the parrots heard
& thought nothing

too   absurd

but the parrots
were expelled
from their

joyous
surburban
cage

to a

v   y
  a   e
    l l

far from human
flattery & rage

and when they gave
voice to their exile

the parrots heard
the parrots heard

e c h o e s
e c h o e s

struck dumb
they kept mum

gave up   the word

for a green
old
age

IV· SIGHTS AND SOUNDS

EVENING
*(HUBRIS
& FALL)*

— resplendent
independent
astride my bike
glowing — "as is
my sunset" —   & ride
smack into
                — hedge

. . . *not*
the ruddy great ball
I thought I was having
— still satfatly
                        plunk
on taut humming wires

— gust of wind
— cloudburst
hurls elemental scorn
on limp lump of
earthen frame

. . . pick my self up
wet through, look
— it has dwindled,
dwindled — to
blood- streak'd horizon

— a crimson smudge, &
then . . . flecks before
the eyes
          flick the page to
     deep blue —

two boys on the bridge
aching for train numbers

reflections on the water

bickering wind   currents play
with wisps of flocculent   tracery left
by the stencilled ribs   of lambs of heaven
or the foamcloudy excrement   of angels, or whatever
it really is   — god knows —
sky wishes   on these
impressible surfaces   — flat earth-
bounded waterways . . .

translucent at noon,   [frosted at dawn,
descants at dusk   enmeshed with impenetrable
at dead of night]   and no-man's land

    . . . from whose
unseen   upper reaches
lordly swans   glide in fleece
to the wuthering kitchen   — flap for food, then
settle, calmly   watering
at the beak   till their whole
heads, and pulsing   sprung lyre-necks
subside   replete
deep encas'd   within
their nun's habit   folded wings

overslept   reflections

— on the cold -
water music —

...as I lay dozing

and vaguely remarking

how each sharp-string'd stab

at the outset

of Szymanowski's transcription

for violin and piano

of Paganini's

Caprice No. 3

somewhat resembles

the sound

of a darting drop

of water from the tap

hitting the resilient

surface of our bathtub

— or of drops

dripping silvery

on the winterbranches

that overhang

and hide

the slow stream

that purfles

the foot of the hill

(on whose side

our cottage

quietly basks)

— to graze its still

faintly frozen

morning skin

— or even [yes I am

going on

about the music's

projected

fields

of resemblance]

sudden hailstones

in early spring

— their resounding

rattles and thwacks

bumping and beading

the wide leathery leaves

of what will later

                          blossom
              into yellow waterlilies

        . . . the thought of which
                          wafts back to bed
                  the staling scent
                          of last night's wine, ye
        Gods! — what a party (and
                          of course, that's why
                      we forgot
                          to turn off
                  the radio)
                          ringing in
                  to us now
                          the mountainous fact
            of a brand new day
                          long since started
            — well under way
                          with the piano's
                  lambently
                          muffled chord-plash
    (so femininely counterpointing
                          the stern geometry
            of the maestro's zappy
                          violin lines)
              suggesting in turn
                          the hibernated
                  lily bulbs
                          — close-packed spirits
            of perennial light,
                          snug in their air-conditioned
          heat-ripening seed coats

                          . . . tho' perhaps at this point
          I ought in all conscience
                          to admit to the suspicion
          that there might just be
                          a fizzling element
                  of pathetic fallacy
                          in some of this ramble
              — for I've no idea
                          what happens
                to underwater lily
                          roots out of season
            or indeed whether lilies
                          grow from bulbs
                  in the first place

                  — nor yet where on earth
    that first place might be.
                  But I do remember glimpsing
   pomegranate-like seedbags,
                  and buds, and creeping
     roots in the shallows,
                  and there is one thing
        I can roundly
                  declare — i e,
    my heart still belongs
                  to the Garden of Eden . . .

        And that's how
                  I felt, as
      I lay musing, on
                  all this, as I
        was saying, on
                  the weather, and
     whatever the way
                  they may wither away,
        they'll surely
                  be back, Oh
      Yea, around June
                  the lilies'
         electrical
                  buds will push through

                  — like real full moons
     shining on through
                  the ephemeral screen
     of pop-song lyric
                  mists and sludge
    — or like [*more* like
                  considering I'm talking
 about the joyous survival
                  of sensitive plants,
        infinitely
                  burgeoning
   against all the odds
                  of unpredictable interplay
    of the forces of man
                  and Superman
       and superhuman
                  'supernature']
 — like original jazz themes
                  after the haze
        of, not merely

                    the middle eight
          multiplied
                    by umpteen
breakneck choruses,
                    but the free flow
          and (what is
                    to some ears
          much worse)
                    free fall
          of the wall
                    upon wailing
          squall
                    of extemporised sponterminus
          variations
                    — till the uncoiled spring
          of *Now's*
                    The Time, or what-
          ever the tune, re-
                    emerges
          just as you
                    were getting cold feet
          and despairing
                    of seemingly
endless successions
                    of far out drum waves
and farther bass hits
                    and dizzy
                              horn spells
          way beyond
                    Anglo-
                              saxo-
                    phonic
                              tongue-streams
          — and wondering,
                    ' — What
          is this I hear?'

                              . . . As far as I'm
concerned it's the wife
                    interjecting "H'm,
          — very rousing
                    music Horovitz
          Why don't you
                    get up
          and switch
                    on the
          immersion
                    heater — "

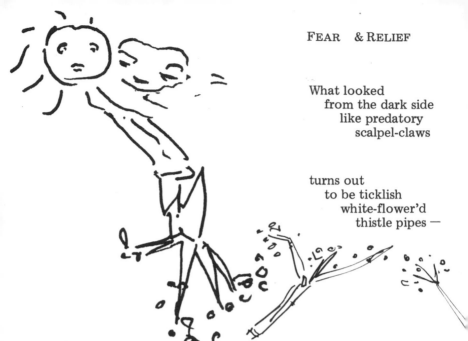

FEAR & RELIEF

What looked
  from the dark side
    like predatory
      scalpel-claws

turns out
  to be ticklish
    white-flower'd
      thistle pipes —

no birds

jingle   in the wind
  starts up
         & your three
bracelets   make a sound
when they   collide
with
    one
      another
like pencils
  in a jar —

A Solemn and Sensuous Musick

(Marais: Variations of *Les Folies d'Espagne*, played on the Oboe, Harpsichord and Viola da Gamba)

A sonorous flood, ambrosia to my ears
O'erwhelms the glittering loom, fills
every pore and cranny of the innermost room
of the Bishop's Palaces of history
— as if Turner's Interior at Petworth
were raped by the supernal force
of his visions of Venice and
the Steamboat in a Snowstorm
and Rain, Steam and Speed
all at once; and quite aside from
grandiloquent analogies with other
works of art, this full-streaming cascade
of sheet-lightning chords
puts me in heat — so
redolent of the purple and
pulsating electric blue
of adolescent religious exaltation, the
discovery of sex in love
probing deep to the dark green
shining heart (as we lay in them)
of thickets of laurel
beds of silk petals
of ruby, peach and rhododendra — the
heavy breathing thrashing bull-madness
probing the new-found undergrowth
of each other, stirring ecstatic
uncontrolled vibrato trills
of twin'd tongue and whinnying muscle-strings
in tremulous smoking-nosed pig-snort lunging
for the tensed and imminently exploding truffles
at the core of your heaving belly and buttocks
thrusting you infinitely undulating thighs —
short-circuiting radio relays from distant forests
and metaphysical rehearsals
for the musical life to come

HIGHLAND RHAPSODY

*In full moon shiny white shoe-polish bright light
  gleaming like picture-book paper

At a child's birthday night glow low as a crow
  gangs the march, each with sporran and rapier

On this night of a gathering of skirling an' blathering
  of the ceilidh of tribes the dervish scattering
  of wildly whirling snowflakes shattering

The peace of the crofters — the solid manse rafters —
  in a splitting of light at the innermeist pent-tight
  herte of the animole night

A White Horse-drawn flight of fiery chariots
  calls me to delight in the bag-piper'd fight

And I write — and The Worde is in sight! —
  it dances to joust at a tilt

And the Word is — Abrraclandabrra at bay — Och
  — it foams at my mouth, it flings its say

Singing: *Skots Wha Hae*, urr . . . See — Be, Olé — Ho! —
  Be — a kilt, with — a   lilt — and aaah- **Hoy** theire . . .

And the Rabbi in me burns, aye — ignites
  stampeding buffalo stalagtites —   till

Haggis mix of McBeethoven Buglebrass-blaring
  lightning conductors' torches flaring —

Belching up the creek an doon the glen
  o'er the fells and the forests, the little men

Go lepping an' playing and working their wonders
    — Ohh volecanic yore-chariotiered clapthunders!

---

*Note — may be intoned in the ancient dialect (not to say dire licht . . . :
rather) to induce 'mair licht' — for "bright" read *briht*, "night" — *nicht*, etc,
etc.   — But mindfully, in homage to the passionately precise word-music of
Scotland [and to its concomitant, wondrously defiant, primeval and terrible
bagpipe music] — and not in mockery, be it understood . . . .

glimpse

muffle of hooves
cracking shrubs
stirring grass

awakens me
to pale dawn
fram'd huddle

— red deer
pausing awhile
in our glade

then (at no signal
but all-at-once) fleet
foot it away

through the brush strokes
of sun
        light   deeper in
to their   forest —

COUNTRY LIFE

— went to woods
to see badgers
— sat silent
listening
heard creatures
moving
flashed torch
saw whoorls
of leaf and
trunk and
sky changing
colours and
expectations —
no badgers —
down their
burrows
— came back to
our little hole
hearkened for
we knew not what
— got shrill bark
of fox that
had gobbled
our stocks

Thatched

I went to empty some ash out the window
still haven't brushed the cobwebs from my hair

City slicker mean wiles prowls
melba-soft on peachskin suede

The blind man stood on the road
and cried   at the garage : FREE   AIR

Football hurtles from the park enclosure
turtle shell glimmer

Red slips sail every washing day
red wails in the sunset

A white feather lifts
ram's horn bellows to the sky

END OF THE WRITING DAY

Framed
In the attic window
Others
Lean against railings
Evening
Sun comes down
Lights
Flare up and away
Flies
Poetry — in smokerings of
Chattering
Teeth and supper, of
Song,
Strong drink to while away
Time
And tongue
Bursting
Cleavage froths fulsome
Promise
Of oblivion in store

V - SONGS OF THE SEASONS

                    autumn's ex-

            foliate   heroes
            bow down
            before the sun's
            last
            rays

                as septem-
            embering   breezes
                flutter
            their children

                    down
                    to ground
                    level

            these
            abbreviated
            days

London's fair
    city spring -
    passed -
        unnoticed
till bare treetops
        scraped the
                bus
                    roof

        stuck deep
in the stillness
        of this snow white
meadow film
        the wholly snow
                        man
stares
        with stoned eyes
— no ears
        to speak of,
jagg'd
        teeth of ice —
his nose
        a lumpen
                icicle

 and snow
                drops
                        all
                            around

freezing
            and melting
and joyously
            re-opening
the strangely
            new
                    found
                            ground —

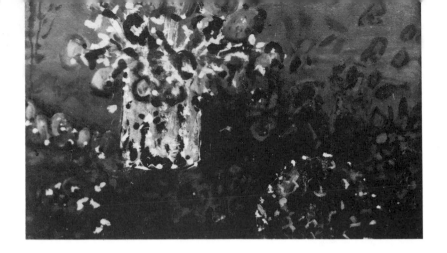

Primavera

   april's buds
explode   into bloom
     shaking   last year's leaves
        out of their gloom
like stars
     they beam
       through   the darkest room

SUMMER

   Red Admirals
big ones — exquisite
pansy-velvet
ruby-rich markings
tiger lily- tasting
tortoiseshell
meadow brown
and cabbage whites
aimless flutter
yet elude
the cupped hand
. . . canny gliders!

Their wild wingbeats

spin me frantic
 — dazed and amazed
to bid join
in mad flight,
sun-dancing
in spite of these
unaware feet
of Mine

 — a slug surpris'd
blackly coils
glistening slime
worming slow
snakes the grass
antennae pointing
mind darts
to the distant waterfall
ripple of leaves
shifting the breeze
to settle on
red ant-like insects
small colonies
mating on wheat-ear
. and rose bay willow herb.

Day's clock stops off
behind a white cloud
and I go back in

and reflect
on the space
it last shone:

 — the map of
these islands
placidly folded
(if Scotland's the head
and Land's End the foot,
Wales the womb
and Ireland to boot

— I'm deep in the heart
runing the roots
of earth-
mother - country
— *'tis* thee
I sing
and salute)
till a moon
re-enters
[time passes]
the room — I forget
to fasten
my seat-bells
to dream . . . . .

A Ghost of Summer

Where O where will wildness go
Now the sunshine turns to snow

The cold winds blow my spirits low
   The high winds call my spirit back

To flow and run — and ebb, for lack
Of clear direction.   Alone I walk

Through empty streets, I talk
To no-one — none else abroad

   My pumping heart awaits the hoard
Must needs reward me at the next hilltop

But mounted to the crest I stop
Aghast — no promised land in harvest there

Instead a maze of prostrate trees, picked bare
   — Derelict dwellings   — Where went the crop?

   A labyrinth of ruined fields that tear
My hope out

               — Unidentified am I
   A last seed blown nowhere by the wintry sky

Autumn

without end

in Bangladesh   as in Africa,
London   Ontario   as London
-derry   — as any place:

the fall of

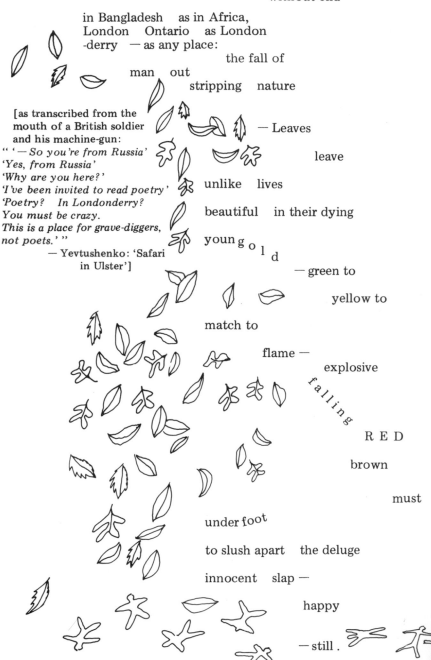

man   out

stripping   nature

[as transcribed from the
mouth of a British soldier
and his machine-gun:
" ' — So you're from Russia'
'Yes, from Russia'
'Why are you here?'
'I've been invited to read poetry'
'Poetry?   In Londonderry?
You must be crazy.
This is a place for grave-diggers,
not poets.' "
        — Yevtushenko: 'Safari
            in Ulster']

— Leaves

leave

unlike   lives

beautiful   in their dying

youn g o l d

— green to

yellow to

match to

flame —

explosive

falling

R E D

brown

must

under foot

to slush apart   the deluge

innocent   slap —

happy

— still .

64

And the ignorant armies, let them eat —
beautiful soup

    . . . as when, startled to the quick
   by a wraith of fresh air, you let go
your tight fist of keys — for bodies contain no locks they
understand   beyond praliné, pramsqueaks on afternoonstreets
paved with paté   the far grass calls, and each call is answered
rite courteously: listen, this is how
   waterfalls never cease
   fumbling into foam ('til
   finally fiefofumfreed for fun
frolicy fish flicker child-eyed) and darting, as chestnut candle
flame speaks in speartips from the nave of no forest.   Demobbed
from early warning messenger rounds, white doves and blackbirds
                                                           jam

and moult together — deactivating land-mines by jamming them
with feathers, and jamming beaks in jocular upsurge to
full-throated incantation — to conjure back
the dreams of rivers inside clouds; whose burst
orchestra winds shake out first fruit -- reborn
renegade artilleries of leafwhisper, stirring
flares of the wild pear . . . the living day
lights   a clearing   for take-off
   every wych-way — flight of the May blossom
or late traces of sticky buds, resins
inform the night, touching on tomorrows'
delicate hailstorms — sprays of hawthorn and
rosehip bullets, pine cone grenades, spiky mace-encased
satin lucencies of conker — branch-hung fuse of secrets loaded
to such a swelling pitch of close-packed tension
as if by order
                  to be blown
                          to mortal coils
— even as the roof-rattling battery of cob,
soft-satcheted walnut bombs, velvet moleskinned
nuggets of almond, pile-up of the spoils
of peace
             ordains the reawakening
of new season's promise   in each festive heart
unfolding   to this moment's sun . . .

VI · JAZZ POEMS

"At home I used to play, and the birds always used to whistle with me.
I would stop what I was working on and play with the birds."

(Eric Dolphy)

Moving Pads

There is no more
       Sellotape   after
these reels
     there is
   a clarinet
     playing
       with   a piano
in a box
   there is literary
society
      and socks

Let
your mind go and become
like a ball in a mountain
stream—

SING OUT:

What's given is static
till it sings out — mobile
it sings from between
the careening wheels
of dandelions, it shudders
to a halt in the asphalt
thickets of Whitehall and Africa
House — Ho hear how it bonks
from the baby's bath, the factory
siren, tantric tea-bell, Chinese
laundry lathe — from the boom
of Big Ben it presents itself
without elemental warning
and if you oversleep through
the awning of sunrise
you'll be hard put to decode
the node of an ode —
   Its clang is the trundling
   milkvan's load.

LIES

     (like
the land)
     all lies
in order
     first he
then she
     order
each other
     about
in lies

     all
guise
     laying down
his designs
     are just
(like
     the law)
designs
     her designs
are down
     laying him

women are jolly
     nice
men are good
     in vain
but a good design
     is a good
design
     (like
the sky)
     whichever way
you look
     at it

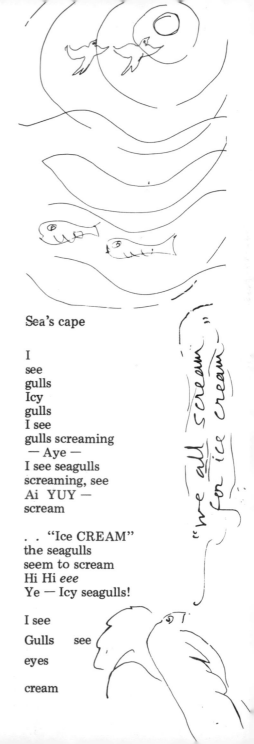

Sea's cape

I
see
gulls
Icy
gulls
I see
gulls screaming
  — Aye —
I see seagulls
screaming, see
Ai YUY —
scream

. . "Ice CREAM"
the seagulls
seem to scream
Hi Hi *eee*
Ye — Icy seagulls!

I see

Gulls   see

eyes

cream

Thelonious

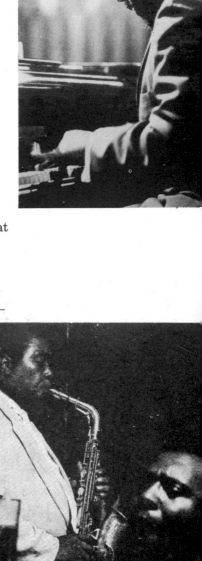

        slates fall
as if hap
        hazardly
from the house
         you build
  so carefully
of scales —

       just so   sky high
       you don't need to fly

       and no more blue
       than pleases you

  — What key unlocks the piano's throat
to whisper through its teeth

  — Blue monkey   in back
of holy monk
        orders
           your aura   so —

light
     sounds   the night
cascading
    light
       black in
          to white

          note upon
        round
    mid- note

      . . . & we hang
      in there

  — sus
     pended, joyously
ston'd
     in mid air

on your telegraphic   harpstrung twang
    till   the lights
                    change
to 'Don't Walk'
            — GO!
                    (— just so
orang-outang   with a cool left hand
and a long arm swang)
                            — With a BLAM BLAM BLAM
    your chord-bang flow
                        breaks   up the standard
            strophe   driveway
. . . drives — streaks away
(your quicksilver path   soloing out —
a way   out
                running
the undirected   traffic
                        jungle jam honkage)
            — treads
                    the mill
            to epístrophe
        — takes me
                    with you
            in apostrophe

to your plangent   scattered   & soft-pedal
    placements
                of weights   with de
                                    liberate
    broken   measures

                            — mindblown
as thrownaway   tintinnabulate   treasures
dumped   tho' still sparkling
                            almost unseen
    (buried alive   O willow weep
    for the roadside dream   too fleeting to keep
    ditched — stuffed down
                        the pillow   of sleep)

— yet glimpsed   & valued   & garnered by some
at the madding gleam   of brilliant
                                corners
    — the dawning rounds
                        & jump
                            abouts
    of streets
                and glades

where you

   lie   (all your movements

truth   (still

   buried   (of mind's ear

so   (still moving

   deep —

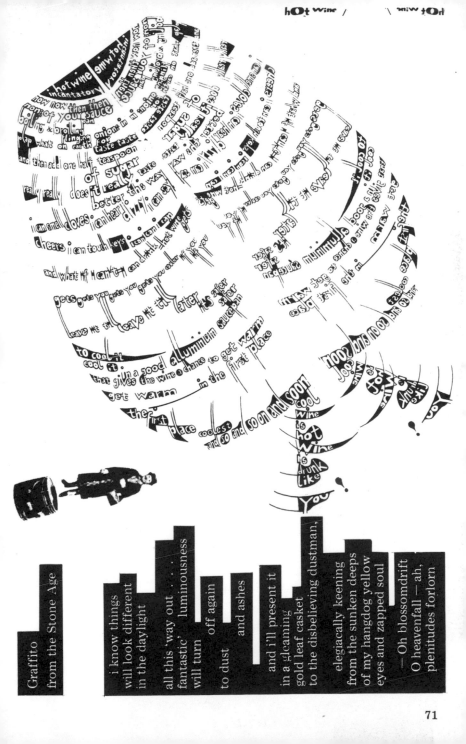

hot wine incantatory

now now then then pot of your sauce
boiling & broiling ringing onion
plop what on earth taste taste teaspoon
and then add one half teaspoon
of sugar
really really does it really taste
better this way raw and
i can smell cloves i can hear i can feel
cheers i can touch keys i can turn i can
and what if i can't i can i can't i can't hot wine if you
gets gets you gets you gets you gets you color of you
leave me it leave me it later then after then after
to cool it cool it in a good alluminium saucepan
that gives the wine a chance to get warm in the first place
get warm in the first place
the first place coolest and so on and so on and soon

cool
wine
as
hot
wine
is
drunk
like
you

Graffito
from the Stone Age

i know things
will look different
in the daylight
all this 'way out . . . . .'
fantastic' luminousness
will turn off again
to dust and ashes
and i'll present it
in a gleaming
gold leaf casket
to the disbelieving dustman,
elegiacally keening
from the sunken deeps
of my hangdog yellow
eyes and zapped soul
— Oh blossomdrift
O heavenfall — ah,
plenitudes forlorn

71

Remembering the Stone Age

. . . languid ironic saxophone repeat
jubilant honks jerk the girls off their feet
and the rust off our joints in the jazz cellar heat
— taking me back to when sweethearts *were* sweet
and the big bhang dizzy spell shell horn beat
done greet us blaring

                  like a sanctified clearing
  carefully chosen by the sun
amid the bleak grey leafless forests
of city adolescence — warshadowed jungle
  where I ran with the smoke rings
for the quickest way out
on rare appointed bull-session sabbaths
— sussed, scored, crumbled and rolled
fragments of afric atomic bush
deep down our lusting unplugged mind-sockets
snorting and gasping and chewing it over
and passing it round till — the moment
  of lightning-flash cloud-detonate
                      tingling —
fused with those long-range telepathic wavebands
  we revelled in vicarious slave-freed glory
(forbidden fruit of the oobladee tree)
jubilant at prospects   we couldn't see
were self-determined   to wipe out

                     the vision
  so fondly drummed up at the time
  — we danced it to
death
  — wild flowers
               wilted
  in hothouse glare

Blank O'Clock Blues

...25 past 11
or 5 to 5 ??? —

makes little diff
if you're only half a- live

— is this jazz
or is it jive?

i dunno — guess
i gotta go scive

...someday I'll know
guess that day'll come

when I'm good an' dead
when I'm **off** the bum

— when I'm **really** gone
sounds like this
'll be my swan-song

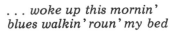

> ... *woke up this mornin'*
> *blues walkin' roun' my bed*

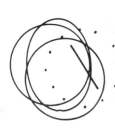

> — woke up **again**   this evenin'
> — still way outa' my head ...

> when I wake (will i wake?)
> tomorrow mornin'
> — will I be   alive
> or dead ?

— talk 'n singin' the blues
like Langston Hughes

— adoptin' that tone
— cheery preach 'n moan

— brush aside pain
like a trickle o' rain

— that cries a stain
'cross your window pane

> ... *well good mornin'*
> *— blues how **do** you do*

well good morning — **mid**night
   — blues   i wish I knew

— when O when O when
   [*how long*]   **Blues** :
will i ever
            be through
                  with you

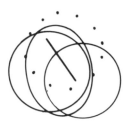

— sing it
         low   as it comes
an' high   when it goes

in front a' their eyes
gettin' higher
            than highs

an' deeper   than spaces
behind   our eyes

— inside our minds
when we let up the blinds

see it all without fear
 — sing it out to each ear

            . . . Poetry — glues your soul together
            Poetry — wears dynamite shoes
            Poetry — the spittle on the mirror
            Poetry — wears nothing but the blues

   . . . 25 past 11?
i thot it was night

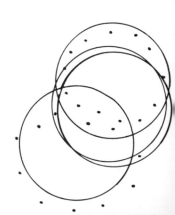

but i couldn' git me
a bite to sleep

so i kep' right on writin'
an' writhin'
            an' ridin' —

a- zoomin' thru clouds like a ZAPoline
 — jumpin' the stars on ma trampoline

of blank-time blues that cain't be seen
 — turnin' grey   to sunshine
      an' old
            to green

74

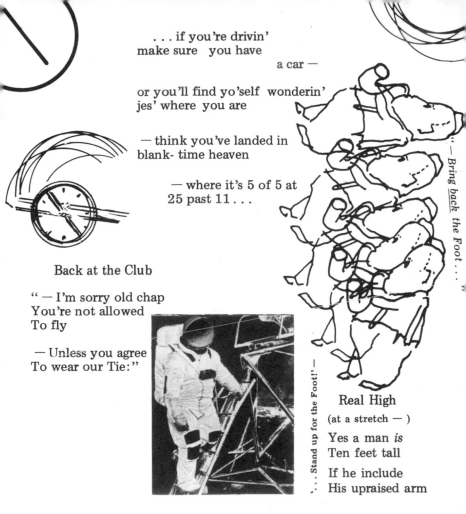

... if you're drivin'
make sure   you have

a car —

or you'll find yo'self wonderin'
jes' where you are

— think you've landed in
blank- time heaven

— where it's 5 of 5 at
25 past 11 . . .

"Bring back the Foot . . ."

Back at the Club

" — I'm sorry old chap
You're not allowed
To fly

— Unless you agree
To wear our Tie:"

". . . Stand up for the Foot!' —

Real High

(at a stretch —)

Yes a man *is*
Ten feet tall

If he include
His upraised arm

Man -to- Man Blues

It takes a man to make a woman, takes a woman to make him a man
Yeah — if a man makes a woman, it's her who makes him a man
But *I*'ll make it on *my own* — I will — I know, I can —

Any man?   *Every*man?   — No man, M. E. — *Me*!
Aah brave man rave man — a whambam thank*you* whee
— Absurd to be a bird — but it's crazy to be free.

We're all washed up, you left me high & dry
You made me cry — but now I can fly real high
Yes — wanted to die but now I'm flying high —

You can — do what you please, go snip your hollyhocks
 — Wou'n' like to be in *my* shoes?   Well, you needn't wash my socks
But if you think you've *had* the blues, just dig me on the box —

'Hey man-beau . . . Go man — Melt me 'til I'm gone
He- man you're on the ball — so *han*'some — whew, some man!
Mister Sandman please send me — a life span jazzman man . . .

'I'm in heaven — wow, how high the man
Can't help loving that man O man divine — ' then
Tune you OUT dead drunk from that groove-juice of mine:

— Trust that woman make monkey out of you —
Kick that man habit man, she'll say & mean it true
Then . . . turn you off & whip you into glue

   — with her Manday at 8, don't be late
   & her Man, you're *too much* man
   till her passions abate and switch to hate
   & you're there just to carry the can —

   with her *Come*-ON, here boy —
   thump me out your innings!
   Hit it hard — give me *all* your joy
   man, & *I*'ll chalk up the winnings —

   with her Hey man   straw man
   What are you   trying to say man —
   she'll drive you round the bend
    — & ride you straight back again . . .

   She makes you feel like Shelley man
   & the minute you show you know it
   she'll put you down as an *Al*so man
    — bet your life on some other poet.

      Take her man, loverman — but
      better rise above her man
      or *What-a-Gas* Man turns to grey man —
      Hang her up — Or pay man —

      Pick her up, and shake it
       — cut out sharp, & break it —
      Tell her: Man a man, go 'way a man
       — come again a man — an*other* man!

                          . . . .

. . . . . .
The sky's the limit
you float . . . you flow
you're happy to come
you happen to go —

If you care
you don't know
 — You know?
You don't tell

 — Think you're in
Heaven?
Well — you'll soon be
in H
    E
    L
    L —

Comes the time when you're *un*stoned — discover to your cost
Yea — you're stone cold sober and find out what you've lost —
That woman who loved you, the one that you need the most:

You've done your nut, you've flipped — you're *gone* berserk !
Gone all to phut — now that ON-moon light is dark
You plan your plan, but how can you make it work?

Your day is done
& what *do* you know —
You come down with the sun
and you've *got* to go

. . . the tabula rasa
of the way out mind
'visions' knock you out
 — and leave you   blind :

You'll come to go & go to come
to kick over all the traces
Then meet, and break — to meet again
and mend at the broken places —

Before they bury you deep in no man's land
'fore you go for ever — make out, make it — grand
Man, meet your maker, and shake her by the hand

 — Takes a good woman to make a man a man
Wake up brother — find her
And love her as hard as you can.

. . . . . . fresh flowers surrounded us

the bright young men
poised at the microphone
night after   errant night
pointing lips to a mouthburst
would shimmer through   mind-ceilings
blast the corners off   every square
enclosed   inch   of cerebration
swing it   gently into   celebration
of the glorious dream   beauty
man quested   ever since   time
interceded   its paralysing   prison
laws   of moral punctuation
I'm still conscious of   ignoring
now is why   I confess myself
still subject   to inexorable
guillotine   curtains
intimations   of mortality
last gasps   on parole
so dance your dance   eternal death
but stay home   why don't you
leave us   alone   together
singing   for only   each other
to hear   till our mutual   ear
and tongues   give over
tired   of symbols   and turn
on   to love   only
turn on   to love

DREAM

Leaning dazed by very wild free jazz against the pavement hedge outside Notting Hill house — completely entranced by the music which seems to burst from the heart of the garden trees — two horns only, blowing so fast, time is frozen, and i stop breathing suddenly in what seems only the beginning of a solo burst — the other joins in to underline a major-key coda — they hold the note until the idea of 'a long note' — time . . . comes back and a voice calls "OUT" : i fall back into the hedge and hear gradually more voices — familiar-sounding — people who've known me maybe most of my life — but they turn slightly menacing, is it paranoia or are they laughing at me (tho' why should they not — I've probably laughed at them some time)?   My eyes are closed, indeed I'm asleep — in the street — *in broad daylight*! Men in cars passing, women with prams — oblivious as watches. My so-called 'friends' continue their mockery — tho' I'm in danger, ligging out here in a dream, with the evidence of their informed scorn openly pinned to me: & now i sense police cutting in from black vans, truncheons raised to beat me.   I look up — and enter a clear completely unlooked for vision of grace — your smiling face above me, & i know i'm here, alive, in eternity — and it's your true self!   — & yet i force my eyes open, and here you are 'in the world', sleeping peacefully by my side.   Then i look up again, and the vision of you has vanisht — banished by your real unconscious body — or more like, affronted by my unhallowed broad awake & seeking corporeal I . . .

Damn your eyes —

your eyes — where are
your eyes?
Didn't they drop down a drain
with mine?

Long ago the rain had
swept us
out to — there, I can see your
fingers

grope at bars, tensed
to pull
your arms your body up — straining
to vault

the void — in vain: you are, you
will be
swallowed.   But ugh — those gaping
hollows —

What happened to your —
Can't you
see, here's a force will bear
us forth

to flow?   Not tears — O, but re-
cover
your eyes, and
we'll

people the floor of every stream
with all
our eyes — the glancing pebbles
  — dance

now, come, and your eyes
become
the eyes of the sea —
and when

the sea falls out to
the sky
the earth catches
fire —

VII - LOVE POEMS

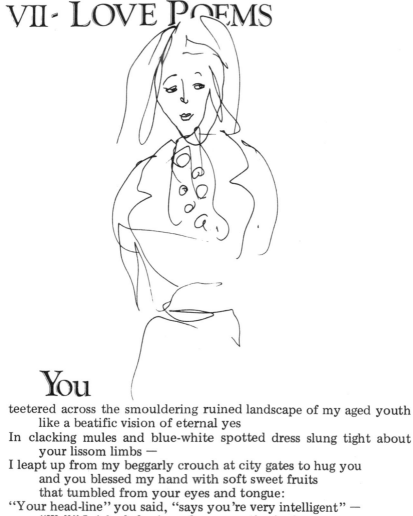

You

teetered across the smouldering ruined landscape of my aged youth
    like a beatific vision of eternal yes
In clacking mules and blue-white spotted dress slung tight about
    your lissom limbs —
I leapt up from my beggarly crouch at city gates to hug you
    and you blessed my hand with soft sweet fruits
    that tumbled from your eyes and tongue:
"Your head-line" you said, "says you're very intelligent" —
    "Well" I sighed, for joy of conversation's play —
    "You surely don't believe quite everything
    you're wont to see in the headlines?" —
But since that time I read & follow without question each new track
    as it day by day appears on the map & newscasts of our love —
Yes — let's believe each other always and rejoice — vibrating to the
    blood that warms your face now laughing through the tree —
In love with you — not with me in love with you — and every day
    we'll trip this lilac woodland with children, lovers
    — angels of all ages
And it will be forever sunshine on your vision.

. . . Is this really

a free love — railway lines —
So that one train can shunt off
whenever it feels like it?   I don't
call that love at all

— Sure: clinging to lines
if it shoots off — it's bound
to fall.   Not alive.   And if you're
both on the same line
you can collide
  or ball
    or destroy each other
  — Or one pulls the other along
    Or pushes the other
off the rails
  — Or look we push and pull
  each other
    back
      to where we came from

— This is nothing
to do with love
These are only trains
  — of thought

— Call it
what you like
To speak of it
  is to question it
    — Now it's coming
can't you — hear
  the rails are humming
    " — Get with it"

— No: I can only get
On it — or I don't
get it.   With you it's so free
  — there's no connection
  — really.   It just isn't
worth it.   So — maybe I have
missed it.   Don't mope darling

                           — I'm simply obeying
                       the signals . . .

                                        Let's not hide
                                        — Let's walk!

— You mean
Let's not talk —

Let's ride!

                   So they did
                  Fast and loose
               Near and wide
          And slowed to truce
             — Man and bride.

               Idyll
               with shadows

               Hours ago
            day broke
                     & now tugs impatiently
                at the latch
           — Get up, open doors
           Catch its bright,
           Let it in — begin
             but No   you say
           wanting to stay
                     shacked up —
                       Love's limbs
                       snug   tender
                       loin-betwin'd
          — Sun withdraws
                  behind
         sudden clouds
             — Gnarled oaks creak
           in the wind
                      & our bones —

Morning, or Glad Day. From an engraving by W. Blake.

(The poem that follows is named after this engraving, but is not intended as
any sort of gloss on it, so much as an incidental homage to what I take to be its
essence. Edward Lucie-Smith has aptly defined what Blake depicts here as "the
soul of man springing forth into the consciousness of his own power". The
poem traces a reawakening of wonder and delight, a single glad day of my life.)

A dawn of agitating winds
dapples leaves afresh on skylit space
awakening alps of cloud to race
& drop out, giving way to sun
as firm in its good morning beams
— A tonic lightening good morrow
crystalling adjective in noun,
name in thing — another day
— another moment in an eternal ray
of running magic rhythm's no-time
releasing madhappy conjunctions
of plenitude — unplanned
realisations
    of being alive —
 This is a day, you say
for visions and miracles
and cleansing of the sights
— A day I want to wear green
and orange
— No — stay naked, I cry, I sigh
but it makes no odds as
tingling to one another
we leap out of bed as one
man, yeh — that's to say
feeling like nothing we knew before,
like — as if nothing *was*
before, like — 'a new man'
— two persons in one
being — animal mental spiritual
poised — in perfect union
of sentient immortality —
 Jump now — let's
out and away, slide down
the stairs Whisht — athwart
sleep's lingering portico — heavy jambs
flung open wide eyes drive on
our twinkle-toed electric glee, dive
on down under the blazing stoop
— toss our heads letting hair stream
wild & free, floating the tree-lined arcade's green-
 gold shimmering budfall blossomdrift
we run run run print our pleasure in
springing foot momentum — touching
 down only to whizz on faster

not quite in step but gaily zig-zag hand
in hand, foot evenly over-
lapping foot as if to tip
all conflicts deftly down the drains'
fetid jaws —
   Lifting by treading
this crumbling vale — Notting Dale
 — called London's 'Jungle West 11',
discounting clerical steps to heaven
 — finding our feet, the day's
and sensing those that did
in ancient time

    . . . Comes midday, you're mental miles away —
slowed, tamed, pacing — at bay
feeding hungry underprivileged & immigrant mites
the vegetable university lies of the land
 — another mind and matter 'weekday'
where mountains drop back
                      to the classroom wall —

   I'm back on the balcony, writing --
studying my hand, thinking over
my thirty years — dismantled, spent
 — after-knowledge of the good
 — miraculous — yes, and the terrible
hours of an age — lashes my spirit,
shackles limbs — to burrow the margin
of memory's heavy page

   — and yet . . . the earth is full
of sky today, and the ageless ancestral sky
on fire — as they say,
paving the streets
               with gold
 — so arise, awake again
to fresh splendours
of measured possibility
 — this super- natural
real world — & the immeasurable beyond!
   Born every day
     — tho' every moment
    the weighed heart
    out
       burst
          its load

— so do flowers — mandalas —
the throbbing universe
our very breath
— all ours — the stars, O love
the only power
                    I'll ever crave.

        Too soon — late afternoon
the tide of exultation ebbs away, so —
I'll walk out to meet you,
      past the glistening panoply
      of plastic & aluminium offices, uptown
      from the sodium-sentinelled glare
      of cheaper, newly faded tower blocks
      looking custom-built for battery, rape or suicide
over the once hallowed ground of play-street trysts
and bombsite chase — the long-lost
yearnings, fears and fleeting triumphs
 — humiliation, relief — and still more
grief for my own child city
                            so barely covered over
      — yet the earth is full the twilit air
busy with rumours of day's work done, this day's
      children home — a moving range
of lamby peaks spreading the evening
out against the night, as lights
flash on in ones and twos, the kids
come out again to play
with ball and bow, and tear away
to catch up a piper
         who's chasing the sunset
                round the corner
 — dancing, delirious with its promise
of summers galore — glad shouts

      . . .   their heads go under
swimming through the deep-end dusk —
long-shadowed cascades
                        hours after closing time
      I see them dunk —   lose themselves
and their long days' journeys
in the void waves' ripple- responses
 — mounting
               and breaking with them
to aeons, where nothing is recognised
 — know death
and surface in the nick of time, riding
high — flailing kicking gasping alive

. . . and know
the weariless labour of love
Blake's little black boy's mother knew
we each
   "are put on earth a little space,
   that we may learn to bear"
is the one undying deliverance
— to embrace the burning joy
at the heart of creation — burning
   for continuous renewal
   of life, the only measure
   of its worth —

   O — let all my safety
catches be blown — undone
for I hear voices — singing, calling, avalanching —
murmuring on toward

                        distant shores and forests
as we navigate the winds and whirlpools
on our ship of words made flesh — your words
blasting open my ears to the eaves
when you turn from dream to whisper
      — You are the key
      to all my secret doors
      that grew rusty on their hinges
— and I turn
               on
and on
resplendent
            in you
                  — and we open
                  all the doors
            unto the innermost
            dawning
                     vision
— wing'd riders
of apocalypse
   — each night
   and opened day
                  revealed —
      full flight

   in the shining armour
                     of naked light

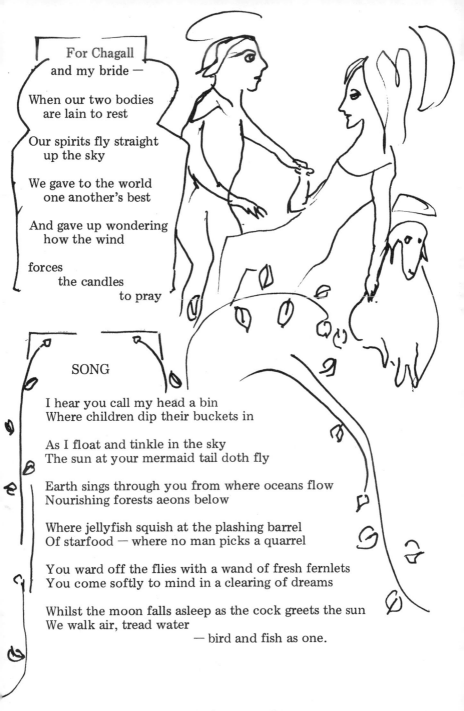

For Chagall
and my bride —

When our two bodies
are lain to rest

Our spirits fly straight
up the sky

We gave to the world
one another's best

And gave up wondering
how the wind

forces
the candles
to pray

SONG

I hear you call my head a bin
Where children dip their buckets in

As I float and tinkle in the sky
The sun at your mermaid tail doth fly

Earth sings through you from where oceans flow
Nourishing forests aeons below

Where jellyfish squish at the plashing barrel
Of starfood — where no man picks a quarrel

You ward off the flies with a wand of fresh fernlets
You come softly to mind in a clearing of dreams

Whilst the moon falls asleep as the cock greets the sun
We walk air, tread water
— bird and fish as one.

The most beautiful girl
in the world is an abstraction
 — you are as old ugly infirm vain
as the next sad man — as me
but the fragrance will always stream
from your warm green river eyes
reminding me even in this dusk
the waning sun is but a backcloth
to our holiest heart's affection:

political realities buzz
at the window, pain is real — yet
much of human suffering's contained
in our embrace; as human ecstasy
whose fountains emanate
crystals of rainbow sympathy —
like rain that heals and nourishes
 — rinsing city dust off flowers
that nod,
          droop —
and open afresh to farther firmaments:

death's secresy stripped clear
in the open market-place of love
given and taken to the hilt —
gold measureless eternity of true
heroic human love outwitting death!

Remembering

a bowl of white   comes to light
   what you
     used
       to say

If you wear your jacket indoors
you wear it out —

to think of
your beauty
tending   the plants   the bread

your two   arms   eyes
ears   legs
waking   waiting
at the hearth   in the bed
so warm   so bright

to think of
it hurts

so   still
and quiet   as snowfall
your face turned
hills into the sky

no no   no why
the eager sincerity
of your movements

move me   now
to ask you
please
  stay
    alive
      for ever

BLESS THIS SPOUSE

O Blessed blessed
blessed be my love the radiant face
blessed O love the giddy ears
blessed sweet love the knowledge behind your tears
blessed the shy, and suddenly sumptuous smile
blessed the fingers that stroke the hair
    thinking it — blessing
      and being, beaming it —
blessed blessed O heap up blessings
on my love loving love that comes tenderly with tea
    and pours forth, and fills up
      founts of palpable beatitudes —
that sip with dovelike gentleness
    at the goblet
      of thy delicate choosing —
O my love I love thee beyond hopes of winning
    and fears of losing —
beyond depth the wells of language smell
Ah love — thou lovely third eye — all gods must to thy
    unsolicited obeisance fly — so be they sick or well
for thou it is rinseth and healeth up the sick
    and maketh the well feel better still —
Yerps thou love that will not groove with gossip-movers to reprove
O love — thy sea-wafted power to softly sing and soothe
    yet rouze up storms if the situation absolutely
      necessitates it without question, ho —
Love that accepts the situation if there is no question
    and accepts the question if there is one
      and provides the answer if there is one —
Love that loves to love, as to be loved
 — Be thou belov'd, yea
and forever blest
    by all thou blessest
      O thou love —

+ + + + + + + + + +

    Doors are often opening everywhere
    Blessing the tip-toes of my worlds
    And worldless to enter the knowledge
    That thou art often and mercifully
    All around me here, there
    And everywhere — in spirit

As in body — Ye super pell mell
Oh yare — thou swellest O'
Bloomiest, well belov'd

                  and perennially blessed

Hedge.

+ + + + + + +

What does this mean?
Why has this spouse turned into a hedge?

— Because she is the long-lost lady of the cake
Who blesses and revives the withered sedge
With birdsong   and flowering light   and an outdoor ledge:

Hedge that withstands the punch-up and broken bottle
Hedge that remands the plundering greenfly
Hedge that announces Spring to the houseboat
And keeps the scene looking clean and shipshape
Even tho it harbour both incest and rape

+ +

                            — Wherefore

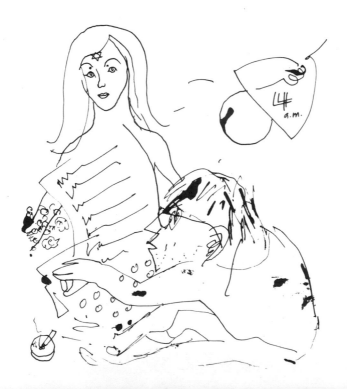

. . . blessed be my love
the begetter of a table
          & blessed the dancing thereon

     & blessed be my love
the begetter of a fridge
          & blest the defrosting thereof

     & blessed be my love
begetter of bookcases, yonks
               — blest even the eyestrain
          attendant thereupon

     & blessed be my love
the begetter of pots
          & blest the washing up thereof
          — *Laved in the flood of your bliss*

     o soul, blessed blessed — well-met fellow
begetter of a baby
          & the sweetness and light thereof

     & bless all warm women
and innocents in true love eternal
          & withal bless the poem thereof

          — tho' this descant be not its real life

     nor e'er that IT can be . . . . . .

Aubade on the beach

Wellington boots after thaw
become keeps to a miniature moat
as the sleeping small hours harvest
romance-blatted bloodstreams for day
   for the sun's ray that beckons
brave limbs to spring
and catch first gentle gleams
of birdswirling light / good
   morning how lovely you are
tipping your visor from sleep —
swelling pink shafts to green
shifting sheet-twinèd spiral
rising rhapsodic from leafshimmer dreamglade
   sparkled sonatina telling
birchwhite and gold
petals film the brimming velvet
softdown kiss-curl garlanded headbowl
   & your make-up bag trickles neatly
kaplonking into the sandbucket / this
Cooltan is five summers old but no
vintage contains unsuperannuational you
   draw my senses like a caravan trail
of curlewing evensong yes —
the call of your heart touches
miles away through the rushes —
   countries away in the mind's goodbye
recalling its needle eye to the thread
that gives its power meaning
   you
are old father sun beams the sea the
eyes the stream where everything begins
and flows and beats at the shore of love's
end rushing on past all ending so lovely are you

G l o v e   S o n g   revisited

   . . . I must go upstairs again
Up to the sky and the fane
  And I will see my mares again
My mares, and with luck, my brain
   And we will walk the skies again
  The Heavens, yea, and the cloud
   And there we will cry our cries again
  The quiet and the loud —

Oyez, let us spread our wings again
   And receive our applause anew
And there let us wave to sparse throngs again
   — Fit audience, though few:
         . . . Be that as it may, to fly again
   With my love and my baby boy
         — Yea O yea, to do that again
   Would fill my heart with joy.

And then to come down to the game again
   Come down to the game without fuss
O yea, we will play the last game again
   And then we will catch the last bus
         . . . And then we will go upstairs again
   And there we will buss our lips
         And there we will ogle our eyes again
   And ogle there too our hips —

      From our hips unto our toes we'll roil
      And ogle and squirm and coil
         — I will buss upon each of your bosoms
      And perhaps you will squeeze my boil

And our juices will flow through the night again
   And kiss us with light for our toil
And replenish the springs of our bliss again
   And deluge with seed the cold soil.

VIII-CODA

Winter is icummen in,
Lhude sing Goddamm

(Ezra Pound)

Lines coincident with the occasion of completing this book,
during Britain's darkest hours of February, 1979.

   In Leyton the blizzards
Are hazards for buzzards,
And in Leighton Buzzard
They bother the lizards.

   In Luton the bollards
Snowed under and scissored
Buzz at the poor buggers
Not splat to the gizzard

By weather conditions
Which have blitzed soccer's wizards,
And taken their toll
Of bowling greens too

      — Though I do not think
   This last fact
   Has been commemorated
   In a poem

Until now.